Table of Contents

Introduction

Raising kids is not an easy job. It is demanding, challenging, and frustrating, especially true if you are parenting a child between two and five years of age. You want your kid to grow up to be happy, loving, and well-adjusted, but you can do without the drama, stress, screaming, or nagging that seems to characterize this particular stage in your lives.

How then do you explain the ease with which preschool teachers seem to deal with their preschool wards?

Your kid scatters his stuff all over the house and refuses to pick them up no matter how much you nag him. He throws a temper tantrum when you ask him to share his toys with his brother. He can't put on his shoes on his own, insists that you come with him to the bathroom when it is time to go potty, and whines about almost everything.

However, when he is at school, he metamorphoses into this extraordinary being that happily joins the other kids in cleaning up. He is self-sufficient. He feeds himself and goes potty on his own. He also shares toys, blocks, puzzles, floor cushions, crayons, and other art supplies with the other kids!

How does the teacher get your kid – and all the other kids in the classroom, to do all these? How does she get them to share, clean up, and learn their lessons without the drama and grumbling that seem to meet with your efforts to do the same thing? How does she do it – and manage to do it with grace, confidence, facility, and a sense of fun?

This book outlines 20 practical tips and techniques that preschool teachers use to effectively handle kids between the challenging ages of 2 and 5 years old. Read this book and learn precisely how preschool teachers succeed in motivating, disciplining, and getting kids to behave appropriately. Use these techniques, and you will find life with your preschooler much easier – and more enjoyable and fulfilling, too!

I hope you enjoy reading and learning from this book!

Chapter 1: Understanding Preschoolers and Believing in Them

Preschool age is a time where you see your child start taking the initiative. He wants to experience new things, explore his surroundings, and try out new behaviors. How you as a parent think and behave (your attitude towards the changes you see in your child) has a strong influence on his development.

How do you help your child navigate his way through the challenging stage of preschool years so that he gets the best out of it?

Understand what being a preschooler really means.

Preschool teachers are well versed in child psychology. They understand their students; this understanding helps them to most effectively guide and mentor the preschoolers under their care.

Take note of the following characteristics in your preschool-aged child:

Social Characteristics

He is still primarily self-centered. He is not able to understand how people feel or the way they see things. He lives in his own world, a world which he sees through his eyes alone. He is also trying to be independent and to test and explore his capabilities.

At this age, your child shows interest in playing with other kids but may hesitate to do so; he tends to be shy, tentative in his ways, and afraid of being rebuffed. Teachers play an essential role in organizing games and encouraging children to play with each other. Parents also help kids this age by arranging playdates with kids of the same age group.

Intellectual Characteristics

Your child tends to think in literal and concrete ways. He is not predisposed to reason out soundly or to think figuratively.

He is curious. He loves to explore – to observe, taste, smell, touch, and explore his surroundings. He tends to wonder about many things and to ask a lot of questions.

He shows the beginnings of creativity and initiative. He is fascinated by little puzzles, building blocks, and stories. It is a fantastic time for your child to develop his fine motor skills and learn new things.

Emotional Characteristics

At this age, your child may vent his emotions in ways that only he understands. He finds it hard to grasp the concept of self-control and tends to lash out at people who annoy him. It is not uncommon for him to pick a fight or to show anger, sometimes for no discernible reason at all.

Your child, like most kids this age, also tends to seek attention and to become jealous. He can't articulate his emotions; he tends to express strong feelings through temper tantrums or emotional outbursts.

Once you understand what makes your preschooler behave as he does, you will find it easier to deal with him. Your knowledge enables you to make appropriate decisions and take courses of action that will help your child.

Have confidence in your child.

It is not enough to understand your child. It is essential to believe in him. Nurture the belief that he can succeed – and he has better chances of succeeding in the things he does. Your confidence in him unlocks his potential and motivates him to do his best.

Do not expect too little from him. People tend to live up (or down) to other people's expectations. Your child is inclined to behave in the same way.

Teachers in preschool say that they start with high expectations of their young students. They expect kids to neatly put away their jackets, pick up their toys after playing with them, and get their juice and snacks – and the kids do. They do what the teacher expects of them.

However, once the kids are dismissed from the classroom, many would shed off their mantle of self-sufficiency. They would walk out, put their thumbs in their mouths, and climb into their strollers. They tend to act the way their parents expect them to.

Preschool teachers suggest that you raise the bar. Expect more from your child – and you will be surprised to see him stretch to meet your expectations.

Refrain from doing for your kid the things that he can do for himself. It may probably be faster, easier, and more convenient when you do these things yourself. However, you also hinder your kid from becoming more self-sufficient.

Preschool teachers say that when they try to get their young students to put out their snacks, put their jackets on, or put their toys and books away, they usually ask the kids if they need assistance or if they can do it on their own.

This question always seems to trigger a child's sense of pride. He wants to show the teacher that he, indeed, CAN do it on his own. He wants to live up to his teacher's expectations.

It is also vital for you to show your kid that you believe in him by not redoing what he has already done. If your son makes his bed, refrain from smoothing the bedcover. If your daughter decides to dress herself up in polka dots and stripes, say something flattering about her "unique and fashion-forward" style. If it does not appear as necessary, keep yourself from fixing what your kid gets done. It will take the luster from his sense of accomplishment. He is bound to take note of what you do – and feel discouraged.

Refrain from being overprotective.

Parents want to protect their kids, anticipate their needs, and do things for them. It is natural to feel this way. However, believing in your kid requires that you stand back to avoid hindering his growth and self-confidence.

Allow your child to initiate things. Let him do things on his own. If he falls while running or playing, refrain from rushing to his side every single time. Give help when he needs it but see to it first that he DOES need your help. Otherwise, refrain from over-helping.

Rein in your over-protective instincts so that your kid will stop relying too much on you for almost everything. Letting him fend for himself will show him that which he is capable of doing. It will teach him to stand up on his own – and grow!

Demonstrate that you believe in your child by allowing him to make age-appropriate decisions. Set appropriate boundaries, consider safety, give advice, and then make your child realize that you trust him to make choices that he can handle.

Respect him when he wants to decide which kids to invite to play dates, whom to call, or what to wear. Doing so does not necessarily mean that you give him free rein. Give him 2 or 3 options and allow him to make a choice – and support his decision.

Preschool teachers say that when you give a child options – and make him choose from them, you create a win-win situation.

Give your child a couple of alternatives, especially when he insists on getting his way. If he insists on crossing the street, give him a choice. Does he want to cross the street while he holds your hand, or does he prefer to be carried? When your kid feels that he has a part in making the decision, he feels empowered. By giving him safe options, you also feel secure knowing that he chooses a safe one.

It is alright if you think that some things are not up for a vote. Your child HAS to practice piano, whether he likes it or not. However, you can probably involve him by letting him decide whether he wants to do it in the morning or the afternoon.

Believe that your child can solve (minor) problems on his own -- and can deal with the mistakes he makes.

Kids are by nature curious and excited to explore the world. They are happy to figure things out and solve age-appropriate problems on their own. If your child does not ask for your help, do not be overly eager to give it.

You must let a toddler fall as he learns to walk. Similarly, allow your preschooler sometimes to put his shoes on the wrong feet if he is to learn how to do so correctly. Give slight hints about what to do next or provide help when your child asks for it – but let your child try to do things on his own first.

Don't shield your child from challenges. Kids are naturally resilient. They don't mind making mistakes. Parents, however, are often inclined to project their apprehensions or frustrations onto their child. They want to save him from experiencing negative feelings. They try to protect their child by keeping him away from situations that may bring about stress or result in "failure."

When you keep your child from handling tasks that may seem too challenging for him (challenging in your perception, at least), you may save him from feeling frustrated, but you also limit his opportunities for succeeding on his own. You prevent him from learning how to solve problems. You prevent him from experiencing the value of persistence and diligence.

Allow him to explore, do things, and fix things if he commits mistakes. Stop your urge to swoop in and do something for him or fix things even before they go wrong. You run the risk of sending a strong signal that you don't believe in him.

Chapter 2:
Independence and Responsibility

Most young children want to do things on their own.

A baby grabs the spoon from you because he wants to feed himself. He also tries to take off his diaper on his own. A toddler beats you to the sink because he wants to turn the faucet on himself. He also demands that you let him dress himself up. This doggedness shows the beginning of the need and desire to become independent.

Give your child the gift of independence.

Preschool teachers know that they need to encourage a child's predisposition for independence. They explain the many reasons why independence is important.

- Independence nurtures self-esteem, confidence, and self-reliance.
- It fosters motivation and sustains perseverance.
- It gives your kid a healthy sense of control over his life.
- It instills a sense of self-value that is essential to building satisfying relationships.
- It nurtures self-understanding, as well as the ability to feel empathy for other people.
- It helps make your kid feel capable, competent, and able to take care of himself – qualities that make him resilient in the face of external challenges.
- It enables your kid to become decisive.
- It nurtures other helpful qualities like self-discipline, concentration, patience, and cooperation.
- It enables your kid to experience a sense of achievement as direct results of his actions. It makes him feel good about himself, a state of mind that contributes positively to health,

sense of wellbeing, and happiness.

Give your child the gift of independence, and you are, in fact, telling him that you believe that he can do almost anything to which he sets his mind.

An individual's responsibility results from the confidence they develop. Self-confidence, in turn, allows your child to explore with curiosity and resilience, feel competent, and become an intelligent and creative thinker. It helps him grow into a solid and capable adult, eager and able to take on every challenge that the world offers him.

What steps do you take to encourage your child to become independent and self-sufficient? Take a page out of preschool teachers' playbook and do the following:

Allow your kid to figure out the solutions to (simple) problems.

You find your child standing on a step stool to reach for a book on a shelf. You see your kid figuring out how to assemble a toy. What do you do?

If you find yourself racing over to offer assistance, stop. Preschool teachers say that as long as these moments seem relatively safe, you shouldn't rush in to help out. The moments where your kid tries to solve things for himself are moments that build character. Don't take away such moments from your kid. Avoid cheating him of the wonderful opportunity to learn and experience success.

Prepare him.

When your kid is just starting preschool, he will be in for some changes. For example, he may be used to having you help him wash his hands, wipe his face, or pick up his toys. In preschool, he will complete some of these tasks with minimal help from his teacher.

Teach him some of these tasks before you enroll him in school. The confidence that comes from readiness will make your child feel less anxious, more confident, and more excited to start preschool. The more he realizes that he can manage without you, the better chance he has of growing to be a confident, curious, and self-reliant kid.

Teach him to be responsible.

You want your child to grow up to be responsible – to make responsible choices and do the responsible thing. Getting to be a responsible individual does not just happen when one is already an adult. It starts in childhood. How do you raise your child to embrace his role as a responsible member of the community?

Start by helping your child see responsibility as a privilege and a joy, not as a burden. Your child, by nature, wants to think of himself as response-able, as having the ability, the 'power,' to do what needs to be done. Nurture this natural inclination. Give him the tools he needs to make the positive contribution that he wants to make.

When you enable your child to help and be responsible, you nurture his self-esteem. He realizes that he matters to the world. He will find it natural as an adult to find meaning and purpose in life.

You don't teach a preschooler to 'contribute to the world' at his age. At this stage, you simply make him realize that he can do good and helpful things – and make him want to do them. How do you do this?

Give him opportunities to contribute to the family's welfare (the common good).

Your child helps make things happier at home – most children do. Be mindful of the ways by which he does so and show him that you notice. If you enjoy it when he sings when he is happy, tell him. When you feel good when you see him sharing a cookie with his little brother, commend him. Kids tend to repeat behaviors that you acknowledge.

As your child becomes older, give him more significant responsibilities to handle. Look for ways he can help around the house. Ask your 2-year-old to put the napkins on the table. Ask a 3-year-old to set places. Get a 4-year-old to match socks or a 5-year-old to groom your pet dog. Invite your child to do age-appropriate chores, and you will empower him.

There are many household tasks that a preschooler can do efficiently. Remember that your child will not just suddenly want to do 'chores.' Give your kid chores that he can do. Assign him responsibilities often and early on.

You don't want to raise your child to think that household chores are drudgery and that you are 'making' him do them. Start him doing a chore by letting him help you. Make it easy and fun for him to do. Give as much structure, hands-on assistance, and support that your child needs.

Again, it will probably be easier and faster if you do the chore yourself. For example, when you make creamy scrambled eggs, you just break the eggs into a bowl, pour some milk in the same bowl, and dump the eggshells into the garbage disposal.

When you involve your kid in the activity, you have to pour the milk into a small pitcher or a cup and have your kid transfer it into the bowl. You may also have to put the eggshells in a handy container and ask your kid to throw the eggshells in the trash can.

Having your child do the task may require you to go through a few extra steps. It is a bit fussier. However, it does allow you to converse, have fun together, and work towards a shared goal.

Moreover, letting your child do chores is an excellent way to foster in him a sense of importance and responsibility. Remember that you are not doing this to get the task done. You are teaching your child a lesson.

Your goal is to shape your child into someone who finds meaning and pleasure in taking responsibility and being able to contribute. So sit it out with your child for the first twenty or thirty times he does it if need be. Make it fun so that he learns to recognize the joy in the actual doing, as well as in the satisfaction that comes after accomplishing a chore and knowing that he did it well.

Research shows that encouraging your child to do chores around the house comes with a significant number of benefits. It gives him the chance to learn something new. It keeps him productive and busy. It helps to redirect energy and calm tantrums.

Doing simple tasks for and with the family helps develop executive functions. It nurtures empathy and teaches the value of teamwork. It makes your kid feel that the family counts on him. It teaches self-reliance and builds confidence. It fosters independence.

Assigning chores (no matter how small) to your child shows him that you trust and believe in him. Simple tasks serve as valuable stepping stones. They prepare your child for more extensive and more serious responsibilities.

Tips for Assigning Chores

Preschool teachers have the following suggestions regarding the assignment of chores to young kids:

Start small.

Start your child off with small chores, particularly if your kid is just starting to show signs of competency. For instance, ask him to put on his cap or to get his shoes from the shoe rack before you leave the house.

Incorporate simple chores into your child's daily routine so that he gets used to doing them. When you ask your child to do simple tasks regularly, you build his confidence and proficiency. Get him to pour out his breakfast cereal or to dress himself. As he realizes that he can do many things by himself, his sense of competency will increase by leaps and bounds.

Assign manageable tasks.

Assign tasks that are appropriate to your child's age and skills. See to it that the chores you get him to do are accomplishable. Set him up for success. For example, ask him to clean the table, hang up his jacket, or put on his hat. When he becomes competent in these tasks, ask him to do tasks that require a greater degree of manual dexterity or competence. Get him to put the table, tie his shoelaces together, or dress himself up.

As your child becomes more capable, build his confidence by putting him in charge of more significant responsibilities. Put him in charge of bringing plates to the sink after dinner, putting laundry in the laundry bin, picking up his toys at the end of the day, or watering the plants.

Do not do all the planning and thinking for your child.

Your child will dally in the morning. Resist the urge to dress him up or get his backpack ready. Have him prepare his stuff before he goes to bed the night before. Wake him up earlier if he needs more time to dress himself. If your child is of the age that he still requires you to help him dress up, assign a couple of tasks that he can do independently. Have him pick up his socks and prepare his shoes, for example.

The objective is to get him to learn and focus on the things he has to do. If he does this morning after morning, he will learn to internalize the process and learn to manage his morning tasks with your help where needed.

Get him to do real work, not just busywork.

Assign meaningful chores that will make your child feel he is helping the family and contributing something worthwhile. Your child will know the difference between work that is real and work that you just cook up so that he would have something to do.

Acknowledge his efforts.

Your child deserves recognition for his efforts to do something on his own. Let him know that you are proud of him.

Teach him that everyone needs to clean up his mess.

If he spills his milk, give him a sponge as you get one yourself. (It will probably be easier and faster for you to clean up the mess yourself; remember that you are teaching your child a lesson here). Teach him how to do it; once he learns, allow him to do so independently.

Be kind and cheerful so your child will learn the lesson faster. Do not be judgmental about the accident; you don't want to make him feel defensive. Put a positive spin on the situation.

If your child happens to spill his glass of milk, say, "Oh, milk spilled. It's all right. Let's clean that up." Get a paper towel and hand him one as well. Do the task together. When you see his shoes strewn on the floor, just pick them up nonchalantly and give them to him. Calmly and matter-of-factly tell him to put them on the shoe rack, saying nicely, "We take care of our own stuff."

Always take a light-hearted, positive approach. You may have to help innumerable times as he learns to clean up his spills and put away his things. Parents, continue to speak a gentle and friendly mantra of your expectations. Use phrases such as: "We have to put away our stuff, deal with our messes, it's okay, I'll help, here's the sponge; I'll get more paper towels…" your child will get the message and become not only easier to live with but also more helpful and responsible.

Make your child learn about responsibility for his interactions.

If you see that your child has hurt his younger sister's feelings, what should you do?

The first thing is to let your child work through his feelings. What made him snarl or misbehave towards his sister? When he feels better and has recognized that what he did was inappropriate, ask him about the things he can do to make things right.

Does he want to tell her he's sorry? If he doesn't apologize verbally, show him other ways to show that he is remorseful for misbehaving. Suggest other options. Does he want to read her a story? Does he want to give her a cookie? Does he feel like helping her with her chores?

Talking to your child this way teaches him that the way he treats people comes at a cost. When he hurts others, he is always responsible for making things right.

Don't force your child to apologize immediately. Discuss the options available to him. Make him decide how he wants to make amends. This way, you allow him to choose what he wants to do. These opportunities make him feel good. It also teaches him that he has to make amends the next time he hurts another person's feelings.

Help your child make compensation for things he has damaged.

If your child breaks a window when playing baseball, loses a library book, or carelessly leaves his father's tools out to rust, show him that he needs to pay for the damage his action has caused. While you may have to shell out money if the damage is significant, let your child contribute his share from his allowance. This way, he realizes his responsibility towards things that other people own – and learns to take better care of them.

When your child finds himself in a difficult situation, do not simply bail him out of it. Be there for him. Guide him as he works out his fears and feelings. Help him find options to resolve the problem. Do not teach him to sidestep his responsibility by making amends for him.

Model accountable and responsible behavior.

A child learns best when he sees how he should do things. Model responsible choices and be explicit about them to him.

"I don't see any garbage bins around. We can't litter, so let's just take this trash from our snacks home with us."

 "The sign reserves this spot for the disabled, so we can't park here. Let's just look for another spot."

Teach your child by your example not to make excuses, keep promises made, and be true to your word. If you promise him that you are going to the park with him on Saturday, do so. Honor your commitment, thus teaching him to do likewise.

Don't call him 'irresponsible.'

Do not put labels on your child. If he finds it difficult to act responsibly, find ways to help him do better.

For example, does he always lose things?

Teach him to develop the habit of accounting for his things before he leaves for home. Every time he leaves soccer practice, school, or his friend's house, teach him to take the time to go over his things, so he does not leave any behind.

In teaching your child to be responsible, you need to nurture his desire TO BE responsible and help him learn the skills he needs. Support his efforts and inspire and encourage him as he slowly makes his way towards greater responsibility and independence.

Be honest and down-to-earth.

Be sensible about offering encouragement.

If your child finds it hard to master a task, give him some encouragement. Make sure that you don't offer support in the form of glib reassurance. Instead of leaving him with words like "Things will be better," encourage him to figure out specific easy ways to make the situation better. Give him moral support as he thinks of ways that will bring him closer to his goals.

For example, if he seems to have a hard time learning the alphabet, set aside extra time to sit down and read with him. If he appears a bit crushed because he can't button up his shirt or tie his shoelaces, look for fun tutorials on the internet. Help your preschooler improve his functional and fine motor skills through exercises that look a lot like 'play' – fun, challenging, and exciting.

Teach your child that disappointment is part of life.

In trying to be independent, your child is bound sometimes to feel disheartened, frustrated, or discouraged. He will feel hurt and make mistakes. Things will not always go according to how he wants them to.

You will not always be able to make things better. If he is not invited to a birthday party he wants to attend or does not get as much game time playing soccer as expected, you will not do any favor by intervening.

Your kid needs to learn that it is okay to feel disappointed, sad, or nervous. It is normal to make mistakes. Preschool teachers say that you have to encourage your child to become responsible and independent by making him realize that there will always be obstacles.

Teach him to do his best and to try the next time again if he fails this time. Teach him to succeed, not by having you remove obstacles from his path, but by his efforts to overcome those obstacles. Teach him that it is okay to take risks, to fail and try again, and to have fun while doing all these.

Chapter 3: Building Self-esteem

A person starts to develop self-esteem from infancy.

Your preschool child already has the foundation for self-esteem. Parents and teachers are in a solid position to build on this foundation. They enable children to go through the different phases of growth and development with a stable and strong sense of self-esteem.

Self-esteem is rooted in a sense that you belong, that you are capable, and that you can contribute things that are worthwhile and of value.

A kid with healthy self-esteem grows up to be confident, happy, and resilient. He believes in himself and expects a positive outcome from what he does. He is also well aware that not everything will go his way. He expects obstacles. However, his healthy sense of self enables him to weather storms. He can face disappointments and failures with a renewed desire to do better the next time.

It is best to help your kid strengthen the foundation of self-esteem as early as possible. It is one of the best gifts you can give your kid. When your kid enjoys high self-esteem, he feels loved. He likes and believes in himself; he accepts himself for who he truly is. He feels competent. He can grow into an individual who finds joy and meaning in his life.

For a child of preschool age, self-esteem comes from the following:

- He knows he is loved.

- He knows and feels that he belongs to a family (and, by extension, a school or community) that values him.

- He spends quality time with his family.

- He feels connected with people. He can relate with them in a fun and satisfying way.

- He feels safe and excited to learn and try new things, explore things that he is good at, feel good, recognized, and appreciated for doing something that he considers fun or meaningful.

Preschool age (ages between 2 and 5 years) is essential for emotional development. It is the time where confidence and self-esteem are firmly established. It establishes how your kid comes to regard himself in relation to his rapidly budding abilities. It initiates him into more complex emotions like frustration and disappointment. It teaches him how to get along with people other than his family. It prepares him to cope with the greater demands of life.

For preschoolers, learning and development primarily includes play and interaction with other people, especially other kids. Things happen in your own home, as well as in daycare and preschool, where your kid finds himself having to interact with other kids. Learning takes place through play, storytelling, and creating art.

Your role as a parent changes during this time; when your child was a baby, you provided him with everything he needed. You took care of him.

As your child enters his preschool years, he slowly turns from a helpless infant into a "little person" preparing to take on the world. It is your responsibility to nudge him forward and show him how.

As your child faces situations and emotions foreign to him, you need to give him the skills to handle these things. He needs to develop skills and competencies. He needs to learn how to manage emotional changes. He needs to remain confident and hopeful in the face of disappointments.

He must learn how to cope with his emotional impulses. He needs to know how to get along with other kids, feel compassion, show kindness, and understand empathy. Learning to do all these will help him become a strong, happy, and productive individual.

What can you do to strengthen your preschooler's self-esteem? Preschool teachers have this to say:

Help your child identify his talents, interests, and skills.

A child gains self-esteem when he can fill his time with things that he finds interesting, absorbing, and challenging – things that keep him happily occupied and productive.

If your child is drawn to visual arts, bolster his self-esteem by making sure that he has all the finger paint, chalk, crayons, and drawing paper that he needs.

If he enjoys physical activities, play outdoor games with him, or make him join the soccer team (or whatever sports team he expresses interest in).

Teach him music appreciation. Play music. Give him musical instruments he is interested in playing. Get a tutor to teach him how to play the piano (or guitar, accordion, harp, or drums).

When you expose your child to sports or the arts, make him realize that it is more important to have fun and give it his best effort than to be the best. Point out that the process has more value than the outcome. Make it your goal to have your preschooler have fun, feel competent, and find joy rather than to have him turn into a child prodigy.

Teach him to get along well with other kids.

Your child is of that age where he is still self-centered. He is just starting to realize that the world includes other people, and he must learn to get along. Teach your kid the skills and attitudes that will help him play well and get along with his peers. Teach him how to share. Teach him to be kind. Teach him how to wait for his turn.

How you relate to him is also especially important; listen to him, respect his thoughts and feelings, and respond readily to his needs. When you do all these, he feels valued and loved. He also learns that these are the appropriate ways to respond to others.

Kids imitate easily. Recognize your position as a role model. When you act with confidence, self-assurance, and kindness, he learns those behaviors.

Let him know that you love him for who he is.

Unconditional love is essential for developing self-esteem. Make your kid realize that you accept and love him just as he is – regardless of his abilities, strengths, temperament, weaknesses, and difficulties.

When your preschooler becomes emotional or throws a tantrum, try to see things from his perspective. Refrain from being judgmental. Make him know that you accept his emotions and are trying to figure out their source. When it is time to leave the park, for instance, and your child throws a fit, he may not be acting spoiled at all. He may genuinely feel like it is the end of the world.

Label his emotions, so he feels comfortable with them and finds it easier to understand them. In the given situation, it may probably help if you say, "I know that you feel sad and upset because we are leaving the park." Once he realizes that his feelings are not being judged, he recognizes that you value what he feels and has to say. He becomes more open to discussing his feelings with you. He feels secure knowing that you love him no matter what. Your understanding helps him to regain control of his emotions.

Show him how to deal with mistakes and triumphs.

When you make mistakes, show him that you can laugh at and learn from them. Acknowledging this will help him realize that mistakes are okay; you can correct them and rise above them. When he assumes a positive attitude, he grows up unafraid of failing or making mistakes. He develops a can-do attitude. He will become excited to experiment, try new things, master new challenges, and develop new skills, increasing his self-esteem.

Teach him to celebrate victories, no matter how seemingly insignificant or small. Help your child realize that no triumph is too small. When he works hard at something and succeeds, recognize his efforts. Teach him to enjoy his small successes.

Teach him how to face disappointments.

A large part of self-esteem has to do with the ability to deal constructively with disappointments.

Your child will experience disappointments of varying intensities in his young life. His ice cream will melt. A playdate may get canceled. It rains. His soccer team loses. While you may instinctively want to kiss away your child's minor disappointment tried-and-tested, you can't always protect him from letdowns. That is all quite all right.

When your child learns to work through the complex emotions that result from disappointments, he develops coping skills and builds resilience. He is learning to pick himself up from failure, resolve problems independently, and process negative feelings. Disappointments help to enhance his emotional development.

It is not to suggest that a preschooler can work through disappointing situations on his own. He needs you to teach and show him how.

How do you help your child handle disappointments?

The first thing to do is to offer empathy and comfort.

Coping with disappointments is not a skill that you learn overnight. Even adults find it hard to cope with disappointment. You can just imagine what negative emotions your child is experiencing.

Kids react to disappointments in various ways: some children explode into tantrums, others withdraw into silence, or become stubborn and sullen. Regardless of how they respond to a problematic situation, they are going through a tough time.

When your preschooler reaches out for you when he is disappointed, he needs you to understand and commiserate with him. He wants you to comfort him and to sympathize with him. He is not running to you for a rock-solid coping strategy.

At this moment, your child needs to feel that it is okay to cry and feel sad. He needs time and space to vent. He needs someone who knows and understands what he is going through.

"I know how disappointed you are right now." "I know how difficult this must be for you." When you validate his feelings, your child will find it easier to recover. If you want to teach him strategies for handling disappointments, save them for later – when your child is calmer and has recovered. What he needs from you right now is your understanding and, probably, a hug.

Understand your role.

If you want to prepare your child for the many disappointments that life is likely to throw at him, be a guide, a teacher – not a fixer. You won't be there to solve all his problems or soothe away all his difficult emotions as he grows. He has to learn how to handle setbacks slowly.

Once your child has calmed down and recovered from his disappointment, help him to process his experience.

How did he feel?

What would he have wanted to happen?

What can he do differently in a similar situation?

By helping your child find the answers to these questions, you lead him to reflect on the situation. You help him look at the situation constructively and find ways to make things better the next time around. You help him realize that he can turn a problem around and make it into something better.

Teach him to manage expectations.

Kids usually become very excited about plans and don't allow for the possibility of some of the things they expect NOT to happen.

While building excitement is a good thing, it is also suitable for your child to realize that things will not always work out as expected. He can fall off his bike or strike out in baseball. It may rain on picnic day. A trip to the theme park could be marred by long lines or hot weather.

You can't prevent disappointments. However, you can help minimize the ensuing distress by allowing your kid to learn how to manage expectations.

Teach him patience.

Teach your kid that many things in life come only after a long wait. He becomes good in soccer after a period of faithful practice. He learns how to read when he keeps at it. This process is how things – sports, art, games, puzzles, and just about anything, work.

Teach him self-calming techniques.

Learning to cope with difficult emotions is essential to dealing constructively with disappointing situations. When you model and teach your child self-calming techniques, he realizes that he can get through frustrations and disappointments.

Each child is unique and has different needs where calming down is concerned. Your preschooler may find one or two of these techniques helpful:

- Cuddling up with a favorite stuffed toy
- Having you read a story to him
- Going outside to play
- Going for a stroll with you
- Creating art (molding clay, drawing, or coloring) to express feelings
- Bubble breathing or practicing deep breathing
- Thinking happy thoughts
- Listening to soothing music

It takes a while for a child to learn how to cope with disappointment. His reactions to seemingly trivial situations may sometimes seem excessive to you. Keep in mind that your preschooler needs to vent as a way to work through his emotions; when he becomes calmer, help him look at the disappointing situation and think about what he can do better the next time.

Chapter 4: Communication

Learning how to communicate effectively is essential to your child's development. He needs to understand people. And he needs to be understood.

Teach him how to communicate effectively.

Your preschooler needs to learn how to communicate effectively to succeed in the variety of activities he engages in at his age. It is a fundamental skill. It is essential for playing, learning, and getting along with family, playmates, and teachers. It allows your child to engage in meaningful experiences, to make sense of the world, and to grow and develop as he should.

An individual learns to communicate as a newborn. He signals his needs by crying, cooing, babbling, and using non-verbal or body language. As a parent, you respond to your infant's signals by providing what he needs (feeding him when he is hungry, changing his diaper when it is wet, cuddling him when he feels cold, anxious, or frightened, etc.).

As you and your baby take turns communicating with each other in a warm, tender, and responsive way, your baby develops a secure and loving attachment to you. He feels safe, loved, and secure. This connection reinforces and supports his learning and growth. It helps him thrive.

Your preschooler continues to experience the need to communicate effectively. He needs to talk, listen, and understand so that he continues to grow, learn, and develop skills. He needs to feel safe, loved, and secure. Communication remains just as essential to a preschooler as it is to a baby. Your child needs it to grow, develop, and thrive.

Communication skills are essential for learning, behaving appropriately, and sustaining meaningful relationships. They enable your child to learn, be responsive, and enjoy mutually beneficial relationships.

Your child needs to learn how to follow instructions. He needs to communicate what he needs, feels, and thinks and how to do so effectively to make and keep friends.

How can you help your preschool child to develop effective communication skills? Take a look at what his preschool teachers would say:

Teach him the value of paying attention.

A preschool teacher makes sure to greet her students as they come through the door. She is never too busy checking attendance, going through her planner, or arranging her books. She makes an effort to pay attention and listen to them. By doing this, she lets them know that they are important to her.

Kids mirror what adults do. When your kid sees his teacher (or you) listening intently to what he has to say, he also learns the value of paying attention and listening well.

In preschool, your child learns how to draw, sing, play, and pay attention. He often needs to sit still and listen to what the teacher has to say. By imitating positive adult behavior, he can absorb the lessons his teacher tries to impart to the students.

Take your cue from preschool teachers and give your child your full attention when he tells you something. Encourage him to share what he thinks and feels.

When your child wants to talk about something important to him, be sure to set aside whatever task you are doing and listen to him.

Engage in active listening.

Listening actively to your child expresses your interest and concern. It also helps you to find out and understand what is happening in your child's life.

Listen not only to his words but to his tone, facial expression, and body language as well. Listen and try to respond in a sensitive way to what he is not saying – the anxiety, fear, sadness, embarrassment, resentments, and other emotions he may not be able to express in words yet.

Use body language, including posture, tone of voice, gestures, facial expressions, and other nonverbal signals, to demonstrate to your child that you are listening intently to what he is sharing with you.

Respond. Your responsiveness encourages your child to share his thoughts and feelings with you. Use phrases like "Please go on…," "Really! And what happened next…?" "Tell me more…!" to build on the conversation.

Now and then, rephrase or reiterate what your kid has said. You will be demonstrating to your child that you are listening. It also helps you check if you truly understand what your kid is trying to get across.

Rephrasing is particularly useful for validating your child's feelings. Describe what you think he feels. For example, say, "It seems to me that you felt disappointed and left out when Peter decided to play with John at lunch. Am I right?" This validation gives your child the opportunity to set you straight if you are wrong or to help you understand.

When you apply active listening in conversing with your child, you also inspire him and show him how to practice effective listening skills.

Always take your child's perspective into account.

Keep things simple and direct when you give instructions or make requests. Use ideas and vocabulary that is familiar to your child. If you are using words that are new to him, take the time to explain their meaning. Consider what your child can understand at his age and how long he can remain attentive.

Your preschool child may sometimes find it challenging to find the right words. Be patient. Do not jump right in to finish what he is saying. Do not cut him off. Show the respect that you would give another adult.

When your child wants to talk about a problem, just listen to him first. Do not rush to solve the problem. He may just need you to listen to him, express what he feels, or clarify to himself (by talking about it) what he thinks, wants, or feels.

Make it clear that it is all right to talk about feelings – joy, excitement, and elation, as well as anxiety, fear, and frustration.

A child who has a "feelings vocabulary" and does not find it difficult to put his feelings out in the open is more likely to grow up free from the burden of unexpressed anger, grief, or anxiety. However, explain that it is best to calm down from anger and other strong emotions before talking about them.

Encourage conversations in the family.

Get your family to set aside time to talk and listen to each other. Use family meals to converse with each other and to bring each other up to date.

When conversing with your child, focus on the conversation or interaction. Avoid distractions by turning off the TV set, computers, and phones.

Chat about everyday things. When parents and children develop the habit of conversing about ordinary things, they find it less challenging to handle significant or sensitive issues when these come up.

Use helpful phrases.

Communicate your love and understanding by using positive phrases to help your preschooler to make sense of challenging moments and get through them.

"I know what you are going through."

This simple phrase, said in a gentle and comforting way, communicates to your child that you listen to him. It tells him that you understand that he is going through big emotions that confuse him. It reassures him that you are trying to tune into his feelings and not judging him for having them.

"I understand that you want…"

When you repeat back to your child what he was asking for – and your understanding of what he wanted, you help him better understand and articulate what he feels. "I know that you asked for a cookie, but I can sense that you also wanted a hug to make you feel better about not being able to play in the park."

Even the mere repetition of what he asked for will give him comfort. It shows him that you empathize with him.

"There is nothing wrong with feeling sad."

Your child needs to learn how to navigate his way through difficult emotions. Knowing that it is okay to feel both the highs and the lows is reassuring to him. The phrase tells him that even if you do not give in to what he wants, you validate his feelings.

"It may not seem fair to you, but…"

Your child does not readily understand why you are saying 'no' to him. It seems unfair to him.

It is suitable for you to acknowledge that he feels that you are unfair and to explain why you are saying 'no.' Say, "You may feel that I am unfair by refusing to give you the cookie that you wanted. I realize that you want it. However, I don't want you to feel too full to enjoy the good food that we are going to have for dinner."

"I can see that you feel disappointed."

Knowing that you understand his disappointment is empowering for your child. It tells him that what he feels is reasonable and that the reason for feeling this way is important. When you simply admonish him not to cry, you are implying that your child is just making a fuss over something that is not at all important. When you give a name to his feelings, you help him feel better about the situation more quickly.

"I'm here to help you."

When your child has a temper tantrum, he feels that he has lost control. Everything seems to be crashing around him. He feels helpless. He does not know what to do to regain control of his world again.

This phrase reassures him that even when he is right in the middle of his crisis, you are there for him. "I will help you by holding your arms so you will stop throwing things." "I will hug you for a while to help you stop banging your head against the wall." These statements remind him that he is not alone in his battle with his emotions. They help calm him so that he can regulate his feelings more quickly.

"Let us sit down together and think of ways to solve the problem."

A preschooler can get so involved in a problem (not being able to put on his shoes independently, for example) that he sees nothing but his frustration.

When you tell him that you are there to help him find a solution, you help him look at his problem positively. Instead of staying focused on how frustrated he is, he feels encouraged to work with you and look for solutions.

"I'm just going for some deep breaths."

This phrase makes your child realize that it is not only kids who need to calm down. Adults do, too. When your child sees that the first thing you do when you become agitated is to take time out for some deep breathing exercises, he is bound to follow your example when his feelings are roused. He learns the value of using calming down techniques.

"I will just be here anytime you need me."

A child sometimes needs space to cool down on his own when he is frustrated, upset, or angry. When your child moves away from you or yells when you offer him comfort, let him be. When he calms down a bit, he is likely to seek comfort. It helps him to know that he can always go to you for reassurance or help so he can pick up the pieces when the storm eases.

"That sounds like a good idea for this weekend."

Even when you say "no," your child feels good to have you listen to his idea. "You say that you want to watch this particular movie before going to bed. I don't think we can do that tonight, but that seems like a good idea for Saturday night." Just having you listen to his ideas feels amazingly validating for kids, even if you give them a 'no' for an answer.

Chapter 5: The Need for Structure and Predictable Routines

Develop predictable routines.

Preschool follows predictable routines. The kids typically do the same things day after day. They know what to expect. They do not become alarmed or feel confused by sudden changes in schedule. The repetitiveness of what they do helps them learn more quickly. Knowing what to expect -- the certainty of every day supports their learning and the ability to adjust more easily.

Setting routines takes the guesswork out of teaching. Teachers don't have to make things up as they go. They already know what activities the students will do for the day. They just have to direct and guide the students through the day's tasks. Teachers may have to improvise in some situations. However, with the routines in place, the teachers usually have more energy to focus on the children and give them quality time. They become more effective as teachers.

Preschoolers are inclined to misbehave when they have nothing to do. Without any prescribed task to do, they tend to "make up" their activities. They talk out of turn. They mess around with other students. They try to fill up the time with unhelpful activities.

Routines minimize listless, restless, and unconstructive behavior. They give preschoolers interesting, productive, or fun things to do so they don't have the time or inclination to simply horse around.

Make things predictable and consistent.

It may not be possible to have the same degree of structure at home. You can, however, establish a level of consistency that makes it easier for your preschooler to adjust, learn, and behave appropriately. When your child experiences consistency, he is more likely to cooperate.

Create easy and practical routines – and stick with them. Everybody has to be washed and dressed before breakfast. Wash your hands when you come into the house. Change into your pajamas first to prepare for bedtime stories.

Your kids will find comfort and security when they have these "house rules" to guide them in their everyday routines.

The Importance of Routines

Daily routines are essential for preschoolers; this is true for both home and classroom.

You wouldn't want your spouse to walk into the house and announce out of the blue, "Honey, drop everything, gather the kids, we are going somewhere!" You would feel panicky, confused, and annoyed.

When you don't give your preschooler a predictable routine, you essentially ask him to drop everything and do as you ask without providing him the time and the tools to understand and expect what comes next. You are not helping him learn or cope. You are just making him anxious.

When your child has a predictable routine to follow, he knows what to expect for that day. He knows what is going to happen. He knows what he is likely to do during specific parts of his day. He is more relaxed and predisposed to cooperate. He enjoys the sense of security that helps him become self-assured, independent, and responsible.

Having a predictable routine also helps your child appreciate the importance of balance, self-control, and discipline. He learns that his day includes functional tasks like dressing himself up, brushing his teeth, learning the alphabet, and carefree activities like free play.

He is assured of a secure and loving environment where things are predictable and comforting. He does not have to worry about unexpected, stress-provoking "what ifs."

He develops healthy habits. You get your child to wash his hands before sitting down for his meals, to brush his teeth, to eat his veggies, or to take a stroll after dinner. Everything is scheduled and organized to make things easy and efficient at home. The repetition that results from this predictable routine every day helps your preschooler to create healthy habits that will stand him in good stead for the rest of his life.

Tips for Creating Routines at Home

Each family is unique. There is no one perfect routine that will work for all.

When planning a routine for your home, create one that takes your family's unique needs into account. Come up with one that is well-planned, consistent, and practical for everybody. Everyone in the family should be on board with the plan. Everyone should understand the role that he will play.

Planning routines for the following activities is helpful for families with a kid (kids) of preschool age:

- Having breakfast with the family every day at a set time
- Preparing for daycare or preschool
- Preparing and eating dinner together
- Helping with family chores
- Preparing for bed
- Doing arts and crafts with the family
- Having movie night or family game night
- Playing outdoor sports together
- Visiting family and friends
- Attending church service as a family

When preparing a routine, keep in mind the following pointers:

- Be consistent. For example, in the morning, follow a pre-arranged schedule for waking up, changing into school clothes, and eating breakfast. This helps your kids expect a certain comforting rhythm to start their day off.
- Include a variety of types of play during the day.
- Incorporate breaks for snacks, free play, and exercise.
- When you have dinner with the family, enhance your quality time together by getting the family members to share stories about their day.

Having routines is helpful, especially for a preschooler. However, see to it that you also have some free and unscheduled time. Make room for impromptu activities and spontaneity. Staying flexible prevents the family routines from turning into a source of anxiety and uncompromising behavior. It helps your child understand and appreciate change and randomness.

Chapter 6: Disciplining Effectively

Like many people, you probably associate discipline with obedience, punishment, doing the right thing, enforcement, compliance, or following rules.

Understanding Discipline

Looking at the origin of the word helps in understanding its proper form and intent.

The word 'discipline' comes from 'disciplina,' a Latin word that means training or instruction. It has 'discere,' meaning 'to learn,' as its root word.

When you discipline your child, you train and instruct him according to an established system of standards. It does not mean that you punish him or make him obey or conform blindly. You teach so that your child can learn, grow, and gain in skill or knowledge. You provide gentle but firm guidance so that your child learns how to manage his behavior effectively.

Discipline is a positive thing. It is not dull, rigid, or negative.

Discipline depends on the quality of the relationship between the mentor (at home, this would be the parent; in the classroom, this would be the teacher) and the child. Effective discipline resulting in long-term good behavior can only occur when the relationship is characterized by trust, consistent response from the mentor, deep and meaningful attachment, and a sense of being accepted, loved, or wanted on the child's part.

Discipline your child in the right way.

Most parents feel that preschool teachers have the art and science of disciplining kids down pat. What techniques and strategies can you learn from your child's preschool teacher?

Preschool teachers say that you need to expect a certain degree of drama from your preschooler. When your child misbehaves, he may not be acting intentionally disrespectful, rude, or sassy.

A preschooler tends to revel in his newfound independence. He finds it exhilarating to say 'no' when the opportunity presents itself. He does this not necessarily because he is disrespectful. It is just part of his learning process, of exploring and determining for himself who he is.

Your child's discovery process may include behaving in ways that you find uncomfortable or even downright objectionable. Your child hoards and refuses to share his toys when he is on a playdate. He refuses to go to bed and screams and kicks to prove this point. He has a meltdown in the supermarket when you refuse to buy him the dozen chocolate bars that he wants.

So what do you do? How do you curb such behavior and encourage his personal-social development? How do you tame your preschooler without going insane?

Maintain realistic expectations.

Remind yourself again and again that your child is of preschool age. Sure, you want him to sit still and be quiet during church service. You want him to share his toys with his play dates. You want him to say 'please' or 'thank you as a matter of habit.

Always consider his age – and his developmental stage. Use these factors to determine what behavior is age-appropriate so that you don't expect the good behaviors that he is not capable of as yet.

Nobody is born with social skills. Young children have a survival-of-the-fittest disposition. They only think of themselves. They are predisposed to do as they please, without regard to how other people may think or feel.

If your child is bored in church, he IS going to act antsy. He will NOT keep still for the entire service. If you make an effort to find out what your child is capable of at his age, you are less likely to feel frustrated when he behaves the way the average 3-year-old does.

When your kid seems fixated at a particular stage, remember that maturation varies from one child to another. Some kids are over their temper tantrums when they are three years old, while some kids are far from over it at age 5.

Be patient.

Your child will not change behaviors overnight. It takes some time. Even if you apply a discipline strategy (timeouts, for instance) repeatedly, it may not show the results you expect from it according to your scheduled time frame.

Refrain from reprimanding your child immediately. Practice prudence and patience. Get as much information as you can. When your kid counters you, keep from correcting him right away, even if you are sure he is wrong.

Hear him out before you do anything. Try to look at things from his perspective. Ask him questions, so you know from where he is coming. Try to understand why he sees things as he does.

Be patient in your effort to understand your child. You will find it easier to get his cooperation this way.

Acknowledge the feelings behind your child's behavior.

You need to be gentle and understanding but just and firm at the same time. When your child misbehaves, even when you recognize that there is no excuse for his behavior, find out what led your child to act the way he did. By doing this, you help your child recognize the emotions behind the behavior. He will be better able to control his behavior the next time that the same feelings come up.

If your child hits his sibling, help him reflect on what led to his outburst. Give your child some time to calm down and reflect on the feelings that triggered the inappropriate behavior.

You can probably tell him, "I realize that you are upset with your brother – and that you are expressing your emotion by hitting him. What is it that upsets you?"

When your child can put his feelings into words, he can better understand his emotions and triggers. You can probably sit down with him and discuss more appropriate ways of handling his emotions. You may suggest that when he becomes upset, it may be more prudent for him to take a timeout, put some distance between him and his brother, and allow tempers to cool before confronting his brother.

Always seek to see things from your kid's frame of reference.

As a parent, there are many times that you wish your child understands the way you, an adult, think. Do you often spend enough time trying to understand how he feels or views situations?

Do you consider the developmental needs that he may have -- needs that he, at his age, may not be able to recognize or ask you to address?

Take a look at this particular situation that many young parents often find themselves in.

You and your spouse are about to leave the house for a long-overdue night out. Your child throws a fit. He does not want you to leave. He does not want to be left with the babysitter.

You have several options as to how to respond to this emotional meltdown. You can get angry or upset. You can ignore the tantrum. Or you can ask yourself – what is my preschooler trying to tell me? Is he expressing a need that I should address? Is acting out his way of asking for reassurance, security, or comfort? Is he communicating something that I don't as yet understand?

When you can relate behaviors to your child's development needs, you will find it easier to be patient and rational, remain calm, and come up with appropriate interventions.

Listen.

Don't look at a situation that requires discipline from your perspective alone.

If you often find yourself saying, "I have told you to stop bickering several times already! Go to your room and stay there until I give you permission to come down!" it may be time to take stock of the situation.

Your outburst will probably stop the bickering – for now. Your kids will stop fighting simply because you have commanded them. You will not have taken the opportunity to discuss the root of the problem. You will not have conferred with your kids about what should be done to prevent the situation from occurring again. There is no teaching or real learning in this situation.

Preschool teachers suggest that you use the 75/25 rule. Listen to your kid 75% of the time. Avoid lecturing. Say your bit 25% of the time. You encourage your child to develop confidence, insight, and self-sufficiency when you ask him to talk about things instead of just telling him what to do all the time.

Be a good example to your child.

Where behavior and manners are concerned, remember that your child learns best when he sees you behaving in ways you want him to imitate. When he sees you saying 'please' and 'thank you,' he will find it easier to do the same thing. Behaviors that your child sees all the time are more likely to take hold.

It is not enough to offer positive reinforcement. Essentially, you must teach your child the appropriate behavior by modeling similar behaviors.

Pay attention to what you say. Be mindful about how you say it. Observe how you talk – not only to your child but with other people as well.

Your child learns about acceptable behavior by observing you. Your behavior provides him with visual messages. It indirectly reinforces the appropriate action.

For example, the car behind you on the highway is driving too closely, and the driver honks his horn. You get annoyed. You feel like jamming down on the brake, letting loose some really "bad" words, or even giving the "friendly" finger.

Instead, you opt to slow down your car or change lanes to allow the aggressive driver behind you to overtake you.

Had you given in to your impulses, you would have given your child the wrong impression. You always remind him to be kind and use 'nice' words; when he sees you doing the exact opposite, he would be utterly confused. By behaving calmly, you reinforce the lesson that you don't have to use 'bad' words when annoyed or angry. You can remain calm, resolve the situation appropriately, and keep everybody on the road from danger.

Put labels on positive behavior.

In the classroom, preschool teachers use praise that is specific, selective, positive, and encouraging. They avoid competition or comparison. They don't stop with blanket praises like 'good boy,' 'good girl,' or 'good job!' They are specific about the behavior or accomplishment that they want to reinforce.

When giving feedback, a teacher will talk to a child and compare his present behavior with past behavior. She does not compare one child with another. She will give this feedback in a natural, gentle, and caring tone of voice.

How does this translate for the home?

When your child behaves appropriately, praise him. Point out exactly what behavior pleases you. Do not be too general with your praise, as your child may not be able to know exactly how he did well.

"You did well to put your stuff away the first time I asked you to."

"It was good of you to hold my hand when we crossed the street."

"I was pleased that you used your crayons on the paper instead of on yourself."

By naming the behavior, you encourage your child to repeat the same specified conduct.

It is beneficial to always be on the look-out for good behavior. If you catch your child doing something kind or helpful, praise him for his behavior. He will appreciate the fact that you noticed his kindness and that you praised him for it. Your praise will mean more this way than if he ran up to you to tell you that he shared a cookie with a friend or to show you that he picked up his toys.

Use stoplight colors to label emotions.

It is sometimes complicated for your child to understand his emotions and how the way he expresses them affects people. An increasing number of parents are now using the stoplight color game (sometimes called the green light- red light game) to help their children calm down from emotional outbursts.

When your child goes into a tantrum, tell him, "Okay, you are now in the red zone. I will come back in a while; get yourself in the yellow zone, and we can probably talk about how you are feeling," or "You seem to be in the yellow zone; take some time, breathe deeply and try for the green light."

Labeling the intensity of emotions this way helps your kid recognize how feelings escalate. It helps him appreciate the value of taking deep breaths, allowing tension to diffuse, and talking things out once the situation calms down.

Be proactive.

Everyone feels uncomfortable when a child goes into a full-blown emotional outburst. If you know what strategies to use to deal with one, things are not as bad.

You can also opt for the easier way. Do what is necessary to PREVENT emotional outbursts. Stay a step ahead by being mindful of specific factors that trigger strong emotions in your child.

Your child finds it more challenging to manage his behavior when exhausted, overwhelmed, or hungry. Make things easy for him and yourself by anticipating these needs.

Plan activities for when you expect your child to be at his best. Feed your child and see that he is well-rested before you take him with you for grocery shopping. Make his favorite handy snacks always available.

Your child tends to feel insecure or weighed down by sudden changes in schedules. Provide structure by establishing a daily routine so that your child knows what to expect during the day.

When you are expecting a new situation, talk to your child beforehand. Explain what is expected of him. Make the rules and boundaries clear.

For example, if your child is to visit the library for the first time, discuss what behaviors are expected. Warn him about possible consequences if he does not obey the rules. In the same manner, explain how following these rules makes things easier for everybody, including him.

If your child is prone to losing his temper, teach him simple and easy anger management techniques. For instance, show him how to blow bubbles or take deep breaths, which effectively calms a child down. Instruct him to take "bubble breaths" when he feels mad.

Planning helps you to stay sane when you are teaching your kids how to behave appropriately.

For example, you find it particularly challenging to get your 2-year-old to obey you and stay off the stairs. Your reason for teaching this behavior is to keep him safe and keep him from falling off the stairs. Keep everyone happy by applying a simple solution - mount a safety gate.

You want to teach your 3-year-old the value of cleanliness to get him to wash his hands frequently. Every time he needs to do this, you lift him so that he can reach the sink. Keep things simple by putting a stool in the bathroom so your child can reach the water, soap, and paper towels every time he needs to wash his hands. He may need to be reminded to do so every now and then, but you save yourself a lot of effort.

With planning, you will help instill discipline; it also makes it easier for you to help your child develop self-help skills, become more self-sufficient, and build self-esteem.

Be proactive. Put parental codes in place, so your child has no access to channels or shows that you think are not fit for kids his age. Do the same with the mobile gadgets and computers to which he has access.

When you are proactive, you avoid arguments. You avoid having to negotiate with your kid. You prevent situations that may trigger temper tantrums.

Preschool teachers always give their students the heads up ahead of time when they transition to another activity. "Okay, children, finish up your artwork. We will have to keep our crayons and sketch pads and clean up in 10 minutes so we can go outside to play." In like manner, tell your child how much time he has to play when you go to the playground. Remind him a few minutes before you have to leave so he has enough time to get ready.

If your child is too young to grasp the concept of time, send the same message in a way that he easily understands. For example, prepare him to leave the playground by saying, "You can take three more turns down the slide, and then we have to go."

Establish house rules concerning hostile and violent behavior.

Explain to your child that while it is acceptable for him to feel angry, it is never okay to violently throw or damage things or hit or hurt people.

Family rules are an essential part of discipline for kids, regardless of their age. They are particularly helpful to preschoolers who are just starting to learn how to get along with other people.

When your child knows exactly how you expect him to behave, he finds that comforting. He feels reassured to be given directions and guidelines to follow. Bear in mind, though, that your child will ignore or forget these rules. He needs you to remind and support him so that he is able to stay on track.

Do not be overly strict.

Discipline is NOT strictness. If your child sees you as being too harsh or too severe with him, he will likely become more stubborn or rebel. It is easier to teach and inspire good behavior when your child feels secure that you love him. He finds it easier to tell you about his feelings and to share his struggles with you without fear if he trusts you. Talk to him in a friendly and amicable way. Disciplining your child is easier when your bonds with him are strong.

Do not be too soft.

Having said that, do not be too soft or mellow, either! Do not "baby" your child when he throws a fit. Distract him. Let him do something else when you know that a specific thing is triggering his tantrum. If he continues with his tantrum, give him a timeout.

Get to the bottom of things when things are calmer. It is good to talk to your child, determine what caused the behavior, and look for ways to address the problem.

Refrain from always saying 'yes' to what your child wants. If you do, he will ask for everything and anything. He will learn to expect that he will get every single thing that he wants.

Do not allow him to manipulate you. When you have to say 'No,' do so gently but with conviction. Take the time to explain to him your reasons for turning him down.

Learn how to handle your child's temper tantrum.

Parents of children of preschool age are not new to temper tantrums. Children between the age of 2 and 5 years have meltdowns. It is part of growing up.

Your child wants to be independent. He tries to get his way. He wants to test new behaviors. However, he is as yet too young to manage most of these things. He does not have the emotional maturity to deal with consequences.

He has a short fuse. He finds it hard to switch from doing one thing to doing another. It is hard to pull him away from an activity. When he has to deal with a change of plans, particularly if the change is of the last-minute variety, he becomes uneasy, confused, and even angry. Do not be surprised if he goes into a fit when you tell him it is time to leave the playground and go home.

Your child is sensitive; he feels things strongly. He gets mad easily. He finds it hard to get a grip on his emotions. When he gets emotional, his reactions are usually over the top.

Do not react to your child's behaviors. Instead, teach him ways to manage his tendency to react hysterically and without restraint. He has to be taught that screaming and kicking will not get him what he wants.

When a child goes into a temper tantrum, he does so for one or more of the following reasons. He wants to get attention. He needs to express frustration. He needs to blow off steam. If nobody pays him any attention, he may sometimes just decide to stop his outburst independently.

If you feel that your child is simply trying to push your buttons, refrain from engaging. Walk away if his tantrum upsets you. Walking away sends the message that it is possible to respond and stay calm even when one feels upset or frustrated. It helps teach your child appropriate behaviors.

It is okay to ignore your child's tantrums.

Your child tends to repeat a behavior that gets attention – whether this behavior or its response is positive or negative. When you rebuke your child or give in to what he demands just so he stops acting out, your child gets some sort of satisfaction from his behavior. He is likely to repeat it.

Refrain from reacting strongly to your child's tantrum. A strong reaction is what he wants from you. Just ignore him. Some onlookers will probably wonder why you are ignoring your child – and not punishing or scolding him as they think you should. Don't worry about what they are thinking.

It is uncomfortable to see your child on the floor screaming his head off and flailing. Do not give in. Do not spank him. Do not carry or drag him and hightail your way out of the place. Remind yourself that he is trying to assert his independence or to test boundaries. He is testing you. While the knowledge will not make it easier for you to accept his emotional and defiant behavior, stand your ground.

Child psychologists advocate that you ignore your child's antics. It is an expert-recommended strategy for dealing with this kind of behavior from preschoolers. Rest assured in the knowledge that you are doing the right thing for your child in this particular situation.

When your child displays aggressive behavior, however, do not use the ignoring strategy. If he shows violent behavior or uses profanity, give him what is usually referred to as a timeout.

Remove him from the situation. If the tantrum happens at home, send your child to his room for a timeout. If your child acts out in public – in the grocery, the park, or at a party, stand next to him and wait for the meltdown to come to an end. You can also continue to get your groceries while you keep an eye on your child.

Refrain from giving your child a lecture at this point. Studies show that silence is more effective during these situations. It sends the message that while positive behavior gets your attention, negative behavior certainly does not. Wait to talk to your child about his unbecoming behavior after the timeout.

Use productive and helpful ways to respond to your child's emotional outbursts.

When your preschooler goes into an emotional fit (regardless of how inconsequential or minor the problem may appear to you), he is in an emotional crisis.

He can't contain his tears. He doesn't know how to handle his emotions. He needs to know that someone is there for him. That someone is you.

When you shame him, make him feel guilty, judge him, or regard him without compassion, he will have a more difficult time getting his act together. He needs to be assured that you will be there for him, no matter what.

Effective Parenting Strategies for Dealing with Your Child's Tantrums

The following are helpful ways to respond when your child has a tantrum, as well as some unhelpful responses that you should avoid:

- Remain calm. Show your child that you are confident and that you have everything under control.

Do not yell and overreact. When your child sees you responding this way to his emotional outburst, he feels confused and frightened. He is so caught up in his emotions that he fails to understand, let alone process, what you are saying. All he hears is the tone of your voice – which is so loud that it frightens and upsets him more than he already is. The more you yell at him to stop crying, the more difficult he finds it to stop.

What you should do:

It may be difficult to remain calm under the circumstances, but you have to do so, for your child's sake. When your child realizes that you are unfazed by all the screaming, he starts to realize that you are not anxious at all that he is acting up. He feels that you are there with him, able to ride out the storm. He feels reassured. This helps him to calm down and collect himself.

Nothing that you say will have a positive bearing on your child when he is in tantrum mode. It is prudent to wait the storm out. If you must tell your child something, keep it short. Get to the point.

Do not try to fix things while your child is in a fit. However, if he is the type to throw things or hit people, stay close to him. Calmly but firmly take the item he is about to throw from him. Tell him calmly, "I am not going to let you throw that." If he tries to hit you, block his attempt. Say, "I am not going to let you hit me."

Keep in mind that your child is not in control of his emotions currently. He is probably scared about how he is acting. If he can articulate his feelings during this time, he would probably say, "Mom, please help me. I can't help acting this way. Please forgive me. And when I am back to my real self, I hope you will still love me."

- Respond appropriately in the moment, then move on.

Do not bombard your child with a long lecture after he gets over his tantrum.

When your child gets over his emotional outburst, talk to him but keep your explanation short. Do not go into a long lecture or be overdramatic about the situation. You do not want your child to get the impression that what he did was out-of-the-ordinary; he may think about doing it again.

Teaching is more effective when it is "in the moment." As previously discussed, a child who is in a fit is not in the position to absorb any lesson you may want to impart. After the outburst, the 'moment' has passed. A long-drawn-out discussion will not help.

What you should do:

When your child is in tantrum mode (or right after he recovers), simply tell him in a firm, no-nonsense way, "I am not going to allow this behavior. If you can't stop yourself, I need you to take a break."

Child psychologists say that if a child can stop himself at this point, he will. If he does not, a break will prove helpful to get him back to a calmer state of mind.

When your child recovers from his tantrum, move on. Preschoolers cannot work out what sent them in a downward spiral. It is more helpful to simply reassure him that the next time will not be as bad. Your child will benefit from knowing that you are confident that he will do better in the future.

- Show him that you are emotionally available.

While it is good not to give the tantrum too much attention, saying nothing at all during and after your child's emotional outburst may tell your preschooler that you don't care at all. This availability will make him feel deserted and alone.

What you should do:

Go down so you are at eye level with your child. Say, "I am here for you." This brief and straightforward message tells him that you are there to stay the course with him. This will comfort him even when he is in the middle of his tantrum.

A preschooler is just a bit older than a baby. Parents tend to forget this when their child throws a temper tantrum with big words and actions. Even if your child has the ability to frustrate and wind you up, keep in mind that he is still a tiny person – and has been in this world for just 2 or 5 measly years.

- Encourage and build him up.

Don't make your child feel small for his emotions and incapability.

"Why don't you act like the big boy that you are?"

"You're a big girl now. You shouldn't be crying!"

"Why can't you behave like your brother?"

Your kid wants to please you. He wants you to see him as 'big' and 'mature.' When you show that you think he is not acting his age, you send him the message that he does not come up to your expectations and that you are disappointed with him.

Your child is likely to feel ashamed to lose it when he has a tantrum. He doesn't feel good about it. He wants to be able to control his emotions, but he can't. He feels that he has failed you big time. He feels upset and overwhelmed.

When you express how badly he has disappointed you, you make him feel worse.

What you should do:

You need to make your child realize that he is expected to behave appropriately. However, you also must reassure him that his feelings, whatever they are, are okay. It is natural to feel afraid, sad, disappointed, or frustrated. You have to tell him that he will get better at expressing his feelings in more appropriate ways.

- Help him address his mistakes.

Do not shame your child for his mistakes. Do not diminish his self-worth.

For instance, if your child knocks over his glass of milk at breakfast for the fourth time this week, do not explode in anger. If you tell him that he is a careless, sloppy nincompoop, you are shaming him. You are not focusing on his behavior. If this is how you always react to your child's slip-ups, he will feel that something is wrong with him – something that he feels he can't make right.

What you should do:

Address the behavior. Swallow your annoyance and calmly tell your child, "That is all right. It was an accident. Let us just clean this mess up. Next time, you can ask others to pass you what it is that you need at the table instead of reaching out for it, okay?"

If you give your child clear and specific instructions and address him helpfully and encouragingly, you enable him to correct his behavior with his self-esteem intact.

- Look at his behavior as communication.

Don't make your child feel guilty about the way his tantrums affect you. When you say again and again that your child hurts your feelings when he throws a tantrum, you make him feel powerful and responsible. This feeling is unsettling for someone his age. It makes him feel guilty about something that he still doesn't have total control over.

It is not helpful to take your child's behavior personally. Keep in mind that he is not doing this to hurt you. He is simply trying to figure out his own emotions.

What you should do:

Your child is acting up because he wants to communicate something. He could be exhausted; he could be overstimulated or frustrated. He could be insecure, frightened, or unhappy. When you can see your child's behavior as a struggle, you are in a better position to address what he needs.

Avoid using bribes.

Many parents use bribery as a strategy to elicit good behavior from their kids. There are many ways to bribe kids, including the use of money, candy, treats, entertainment, or toys to make them do what you want.

It can be tempting to resort to bribery. The response is almost immediate. If you dangle an attractive bribe before your child's nose, he is quick to take the bait and do what you want him to. No stress, no nagging, no waiting – which parent does not want this? But is bribery prudent?

Many parenting educators and child counselors do not seem to think so. Bribery tends to send a wrong message to a child, especially one who is of preschool age. It suggests that engaging in the behavior in question is not fundamentally rewarding; it does not have any real intrinsic value. Otherwise, why is there a need to bribe, to 'pay' the child to do it?

A bribe makes your child hyper-focus on the 'prize,' which is an external motivator. He fails to appreciate the internal motivator – the pride, sense of accomplishment, or satisfaction from behaving appropriately.

If your child does his homework because you have promised him a treat, if he does so, he is likely to rush through the task just to get the pleasure. He isn't likely to take pride in doing the task because it is the right thing to do or to do it the best way he can, for that matter. He does not get to feel the sense of accomplishment that comes from doing a job well.

A bribe is essentially a quick fix. It does not make the child learn something of value. It does not impress on him the intrinsic rewards of good behavior. It does not teach him responsibility or respect. It may even help foster a sense of entitlement.

When you make it a habit to use bribes, you condition your preschooler to think that he is entitled to something good each time he does something you ask him to do. He completes his homework or picks up his toys because of the incentive attached to these behaviors. He regards the behavior as a choice – something he has to do if he wants the treat. If he finds the treat not motivating enough, he simply refuses to do what is asked of him.

When you condition your child to expect a treat for good behavior, he learns to expect more. It is similar to using pain medication. It works well at first. As you get used to it, however, it becomes less effective. You need a more significant dose to feel its effects.

Bribery results in satiation. It causes what is referred to as 'upping the ante.'

As your child gets used to treats, he learns to hold out for even bigger ones. He is learning to refuse to do what you ask of him if you do not promise a bigger or better treat.

Bribery brings about only short-term results. It elicits temporary compliance. It makes your child overly dependent on promised treats to motivate him. It fails to foster long-term good behavior, autonomy, competence, and inner satisfaction.

When you bribe your child to do as you want, you 'teach' him to control and manipulate – because that is what you, yourself, are doing. You are using control tactics. You are using bribes to manage your child's behavior. If he does not do as you say, you withhold the treat; this is manipulation. You are not helping your child develop a sense of personal responsibility towards the chores or tasks you want him to do. You are 'managing' his behavior.

Bribery and Rewarding Good Behavior

It is prudent to understand the thin line between bribery and rewarding his good behavior.

Bribery is offered to stop your child from continuing inappropriate behavior. He refuses to do his homework. He does not want to go to school. He has a temper tantrum. You want to stop him from continuing these behaviors, so you bribe him to change tack.

For example, you have to leave the park. Your child does not want to go, and he throws a temper tantrum. You offer him an ice cream cone so he will stop acting out; this is bribery.

On the other hand, your child picks up his toys and puts them away – without being asked. You acknowledge his good behavior, praise him for it, and give him candy. You reward his behavior.

Child psychologists suggest you expect and praise certain behaviors like proper personal hygiene, respect, and good manners. Do not bribe your children to engage in these behaviors.

When you see your child trying his best to rise above past behavioral struggles, work hard to excel, be extra thoughtful without being asked, then giving a reward may help encourage him to continue with good behavior.

Giving a reward does not necessarily mean giving your child something material. The reward can come in the form of making him feel good about himself.

Your preschooler is more predisposed to cooperate when he feels confident, capable, and important. Spend time to build your child's confidence in his ability to do the right thing. For instance, after he works hard on his assignment, you may want to say, "It must feel good to finish your homework finally; you worked so hard on it!"

Show your child that you notice and appreciate it when he does something nice over and above what you expect from him.

There is nothing wrong with expressing genuine appreciation if your child goes out of his way to do something good. For example, if your child organizes his things and cleans his entire room, you can tell him something like, "I am pleased about what you did. It was such a nice and thoughtful thing to do! What do you think about going to the kitchen to whip up a batch of brownies with me? That would be fun!"

It is important to note that you are showing appreciation for good behavior after the fact. Your preschooler did not behave as he did because he wanted a reward. He did it because it was the right thing to do or because he sincerely wanted to do something that would please you.

Chapter 7: Stop Yelling at Your Kids

When is it okay to yell?

You yell when you are excited or overjoyed. You also yell when you see your child about to walk into the road, fall off the bicycle, or touch a hot stove; you yell to express panic, as well as to get your child's attention and get him to safety. It is okay to yell for these reasons.

Do not yell to teach your child to behave appropriately.

When it comes to teaching your preschool-aged child appropriate behaviors, child development specialists and parenting counselors agree that yelling seldom works.

Parenting is tough. It calls for understanding, kindness, compassion, patience, restraint, strength of mind, and self-discipline. Many parents compare parenting to walking through a minefield. You can't predict the next explosion.

Parents yell for a variety of reasons. Some see yelling as an old-school way of instilling discipline. Most yell because they lose their cool.

It is challenging to raise preschoolers. The job can get pretty exhausting and frustrating – and parents sometimes just kind of let go in reaction. The frustration or anger seems to just sneak in without your knowledge. It hijacks you in a manner of speaking, and you scream or yell to try to get your children to behave.

Your preschooler has meltdowns for reasons that sometimes seem like only he can understand. He refuses to listen to you. He makes you go crazy. When you let your emotions – frustration, exhaustion, or hopelessness, get the better of you, you find yourself yelling your head off. But when you do, you are just allowing yourself to have a meltdown just like your kids. You are not helping your child nor yourself any. You are only making the situation worse.

Do not let your preschooler's behavior push you over the edge. Remember that he cannot, as yet, find the language to express his emotions, control his impulses, or regulate his behavior. He whines or goes into a temper tantrum when he is overstimulated or experiences strong emotions that he frequently doesn't understand. He does not have the ability or skills to remain calm and collected. When you yell at him, it serves no positive purpose. It is not a good strategy for conflict-resolution. It does not make things better; it can even make things worse.

When you yell at your kid, it often frightens him. It makes him anxious. He feels scared and intimidated. You may get him to behave the way you want to –and finally stop whining or fighting, for example, but the behavior change is just a result of your child's desire to make you stop yelling. It is not because he has finally realized that whining or fighting is not appropriate behavior and wants to change it.

Yelling may seem effective in changing your child's behavior, but it only works in the short term. If you continue using this approach, your child will tune it out, shut down, or withdraw. He may even learn to yell more himself.

You hardly see preschool teachers yelling at their students. Take a leaf out of their book and use the following steps to learn the art of NOT yelling.

Recognize your triggers.

You yell because something triggers you. It is a response to something. Find out what your triggers are and do something about them.

For instance, you usually have a short fuse when you come home at the end of the day. You are exhausted. You feel stressed from work. You feel frustrated because you are too tired to make dinner. As a result, you tend to yell at your kid for the slightest misdemeanor.

Self-awareness enables you to do something so that you don't quickly lose your cool. Distract your kid by giving him blocks to play with or a good show to watch so you can cook in peace. Pour yourself a cocktail and try to relax before starting dinner. Make simple and healthy sandwiches for dinner.

Warn your kids.

Give your kids the heads up when you are feeling provoked. When your irritation mounts as they fight in the car or stall bedtime, give them enough warning. For example, tell them, "Hey. I'm about to lose it. Don't push me. You better stop bickering; you don't want to push me." When you give this warning in a calm but firm voice, it is usually enough to get kids to obey you and tone things down.

Giving fair warning is also an excellent way to get kids to prepare for change. When they are too engrossed at play to heed your request for them to get ready for bed, give them the heads up. Say, "Okay, I really mean it. I'm giving you five more minutes to play. That is all I can handle, so you better wrap things up before I lose my cool."

Practice restraint by giving yourself a timeout.

Go to the bathroom, yell at the walls, and flush your anger down the toilet. This calm-down technique seems effective for a lot of adults. It allows you to leave the room, vent your irritation at something other than your kids, and compose yourself. If it works for you, squeeze a stress ball. Send your spouse to deal with your kids. The important thing is to take a timeout before you do anything. It helps you to control your impulses and mindfully change your disposition and behavior.

Make a list of acceptable behaviors to warn you are about to yell or do something you are bound to regret.

It is a good idea to sit down with your family to discuss and draw up this list so that everyone is on board about it. Make a list and tape it on the wall where everyone can see it as a reminder. Behaviors may include

- Announcing to everybody that you are going to the bathroom to do some deep breathing
- Jogging in place
- Squeezing the stress ball
- Counting from 1 to 100
- Bouncing a ball

When the kids pick up on what you are doing, it reminds them to mind their ways. They may also learn to engage in these acceptable behaviors when they find themselves about to blow up.

Wait to teach the lesson.

When you try to impart a lesson right after your kids misbehave, you tend to shout or yell. Your kids are not likely to listen and absorb what you want them to learn.

Wait for the heat of the moment to die down before talking to your kids. The lull will help you regain self-control. When your kids see you practicing self-restraint, it sends them a more strong message.

After everybody has calmed down, ask why your kids behaved the way they did. Explain why you are displeased. Remind them how you expect them to behave and the consequences of inappropriate behavior.

Solve the problem.

Did your kids make a mess? Have them clean it up; help them when they need your assistance. Was your daughter impertinent? Ask her why she was disrespectful (Did she have a difficult or tiring day?). Discuss why her behavior is inappropriate and how she could have behaved better.

Remind yourself what behaviors are normal for preschoolers.

This reminder enables you to put things in perspective. When your child whines, resists going to bed on time, or always demands your attention, knowing that these behaviors are common to preschoolers keeps you from reacting too strongly.

Remind yourself that your child is not behaving the way he does just to make you mad. He is dealing with behavioral predispositions normal for kids his age. Remember this, and you find yourself getting angry and yelling less frequently.

Be proactive.

If the morning rush always triggers a shouting match, take some of the edge off by prepping the night before. Get clothes and backpacks ready to go. Wake up earlier to prepare and eat breakfast.

Do your kids whine because they get hungry in the middle of your afternoon walk? Always bring along some convenient snacks for them. When you take them with you when you run errands, do they always pick fights with each other? Take toys and board games for your kids, so they don't get on each other's nerves from boredom.

Be proactive and see the big difference it makes in everyone's disposition.

Modify your expectations.

When your child fails to deliver as expected, do you get dismally disappointed? Do you feel like a parental failure? These feelings tend to make you yell. Save yourself from frustration by keeping your expectations realistic.

Go for a shorter walk. Make fewer and shorter errands when you take the kids with you. Give out instructions one at a time. Prepare to abandon all expectations when things go south. Give your child and yourself a lot of leeway.

Make out when the problem is you and not your child.

Is work stress getting the better of you? Do you and your spouse have issues to thresh out? Are you overworked?

Sometimes, yelling has more to do with you than with your misbehaving child. Sometimes you yell because you have unmet needs or personal problems that have nothing to do with him.

Ask yourself if other things are going on with you. Are you getting enough sleep? Do you feel that your husband (or friends or co-workers or boss) does not appreciate you enough? If you get to the root of your problem and resolve it, you may suddenly realize that you don't yell at your child anymore.

Do not hesitate to make things right.

When you realize that your child did not in any way deserve to have you yell your head off at him, what do you do? Experts suggest that you apologize.

How do you go about repairing the situation? You may find this formula helpful:

1. Recognize your mistake; own up to your feelings, and accept that you are responsible for managing (or failing to address) them.

It's okay to feel upset or become frustrated sometimes; you tell your child this again and again. Just keep in mind that the way you express your emotions may not always be okay. Yelling and slamming doors are not appropriate ways to express your feelings. Your child takes his cue on how to behave from you. Don't act in ways that you don't want him to emulate.

2. Make the connection between how you felt and how you behaved.

When you apologize, explain to your child what triggered you into yelling. You don't want to put blame anywhere; you simply want to explain how and why you felt that way in that particular situation. Your child needs to understand the cause and effect relationship between feelings and actions.

3. Apologize.

Identify your inappropriate behavior and explain why it is unacceptable. By doing this, you are teaching your child that it is wrong for him to behave this way, too.

4. Acknowledge your child's feelings.

Show your child that you understand that he felt frightened or hurt by your yelling. Even if your behavior was triggered by something your child did or failed to do, help him know that it wasn't right for you to react that way. Assure him that you love him.

5. Discuss with him how you intend to avoid having the same thing happen in the future.

Share with your child what specific steps you plan to take not to yell or lose it again in the future. This opportunity is a good occasion for teaching how a person can learn from the mistakes he makes, make amends, and improve himself.

6. Ask your child to forgive you.

Make it simple and direct. A straightforward "Can you please forgive me for acting as I did?" helps make your child and yourself feel better.

7. Keep the focus on solutions.

Not all situations are about you losing control; some may involve your child's need to modify his behavior.

If this is the case, do not make it just about your child and his role in triggering your inappropriate behavior. Apply the team approach. Your child's behavior has set you off. What can both of you do to resolve things? Talk about the things each of you can do so that the same thing does not happen again.

A make-things-right apology may look something like this:

"I really felt upset that you were not ready to leave for school on time. I felt frustrated and angry because I did not want you to be late for school. But I let my frustration out by yelling at you – which I shouldn't have done. It was not okay for me to do that. I am sorry to lose control of my emotions. I know that you felt scared and hurt by my yelling.

I realize that I need to be calmer. I am going to post reminders around the house so that I'd remember to act more appropriately. Please forgive me?

I would like for us to talk about how we can both do better so that this does not happen again."

When you sincerely are sorry for acting out and admit it to your child, your apology helps in many ways.

- It reminds your child that you are only human and that you make mistakes.

- It teaches your child that when a person allows emotions to rule him, these emotions may lead him to talk or act in unhelpful ways.

- It makes things right; it takes the sting out of an unpleasant and hurtful situation.

- By modeling the appropriate behavior, you teach your child the right thing to do when he hurts others by losing his temper.

- It tells your child that if he makes mistakes, he can always choose to make things right.

Chapter 8:
Teaching Manners to Your Preschooler

How polite, friendly, and well-mannered should your preschooler be? This is hard to know.

A significant level of self-centeredness characterizes preschool age. However, it is also the stage where your child does not want to be seen as a 'baby' anymore. He wants to be treated as a 'person,' as an adult.

Thus, it is an excellent time to teach your child to mind his manners, be nice, as adults are, and treat other people like adults do – with the respect and kindness that they deserve. It also helps that this is a stage where your child naturally wants to please you.

Teach your child to treat people well.

How do you develop a preschooler's sense of decorum and social graces? You may want to start with helping him develop the following habits:

Being kind

In preschool, your kid's teacher tries to instill certain behaviors in children, both in the classroom and on the playground. Be friendly. Share. Take turns. Be kind. Be nice. You may call these precepts the 'law of the land.'

When you see other people, especially kids, exhibit the behaviors you would like to instill in your kid, point these behaviors out to your kid. Make him aware of people doing nice and sweet things for other people – and he will realize the value of the actions you are pointing out to him and start to identify with and imitate them.

Your preschool kid is still possessive and self-centered; he finds it hard and uncomfortable to let someone else play with his toys. You have to remind and encourage him to do so constantly.

Be understanding and sympathetic. Show great enthusiasm when your child gives a friend a turn on his bicycle or lends his toys to other kids. When you praise him, you make him want to do it and get your praise, again and again, until kindness becomes a habit.

Saying "please" and "thank you."

Simple niceties reflect good manners, and they make people feel good.

Teach your child the habit of saying "please" and "thank you." These 'magic words' are fundamental to social graces.

Routinely remind your child to say "please" when he asks someone to do anything for him – and to say "thank you" to everyone who helps him with anything, serves him food, gives him a present, or does anything friendly or thoughtful for him. Point out how this simple and straightforward habit makes people, including Mom and Dad, feel good and shows others that you respect and appreciate them.

Greeting people properly

Teach your child how to address an adult (to use 'Mr.' or 'Ms' where appropriate) and how to greet someone appropriately.

You may have to be content to coax a dutiful "Hello" from your child in the beginning. As he feels more comfortable with the introductory greeting, teach him to face the person directly and look him in the eye. Asking your child if he noticed the other person's eye color makes the habit fun and strengthens it.

Move on to the next step, the handshake. Demonstrate what makes a friendly, firm handshake different from a 'dead fish' or a weak handshake. Help your child get used to saying, "How do you do?" and "I'm fine, thank you."

Do some role-playing at home. Practice introductions using pretend-characters and make it fun for your child to learn these social skills.

Not interrupting

Teach your child to wait for his turn to speak. Many preschoolers find this hard to do. They want to be able to express right away what comes to their minds. By nature, they are still self-centered and need to be reminded not to interrupt, wait, and let the other person finish what he is saying.

Some preschool teachers use a visual reminder of a talking stick or stuffed toy to teach this lesson. The teacher gives the stick to a kid, and everybody stays silent when that kid is speaking. Another kid gets his turn to speak when the teacher gives him the stick. The stick reminds the kids to wait for their turn and not interrupt. It teaches them to be patient.

When you are on the phone with another person, and your child insists on getting your immediate attention, explain to him firmly that it is never okay to interrupt. (It is only acceptable to interrupt when he needs to go potty right now, when he or someone is hurt and needs mommy's attention, or when something similarly critical happens). Show him things he can do (play with blocks, for instance) to keep him occupied while he waits for you. When you finish your call, thank your child for his patience. Tell him that it is his turn now and listen to him with undivided attention.

Practicing good manners when eating

Help your child to learn basic table manners. Teach him to wait until everyone is also served before eating. Teach him not to chew loudly or to chew with his mouth open. Teach him to say "please" when asking for food or water and "thank you" after he is served. Even a 2-year-old will be able to follow these simple rules.

Teach an older child how to put a napkin on his lap correctly. Teach him to converse pleasantly with others.

Your preschooler will find it hard to stay put on his chair -- without toys or television, for the entire duration of the family dinner. However, you can expect a 3-year-old to be able to do this for 10 minutes. Work your way up until your child gets used to the practice.

Make it easy for your child to get used to and enjoy family dinner by establishing a consistent and cheerful routine.

- Have dinner at the same time every night.
- Do not give your child snacks or juice just before dinner so that he is hungry enough to enjoy having dinner with the family.
- Make it a rule for everybody to eat only at the table.
- Turn off the TV.

- Do not allow anyone to bring their cell phones to the table.

Use dinner time as an opportunity for the kids to practice good manners – listening with interest, waiting for their turn to speak, conversing pleasantly, and improving their social skills.

Going on playdates

When your preschooler goes on playdates, teach him the simple niceties –

- To greet his host respectfully
- To be courteous and polite
- To observe the rules of the house
- To speak in a pleasant, not too loud voice
- Not to put his feet up on the furniture
- Not to eat ahead of the host when offered snacks
- To say "please" and "thank you."
- To clean up after himself before he leaves
- To thank his host before leaving

When it is your child's turn to play host, teach him to be a gracious host –

- To lend his toys
- To serve his guest first
- To make sure his guest has a nice time

It is challenging to teach a child good manners if you don't practice them yourself. Be mindful of your behavior. You set the standards for your child. If you want to raise a courteous, respectful, and well-mannered child, be consistent in practicing good manners yourself.

Chapter 9: Play and Fun

Play is fundamental to a preschooler's growth and development.

If you want your preschooler to grow up healthy, bright, creative, curious, and happy, give him time to play.

Let him laugh and blow bubbles in his milk. Get him to jump, run, chase, and play hide-and-seek. Get him to pretend to be a pirate. Let him have a go at the slide or the swing in the playground. Let him play.

Play is an essential element in learning. A preschooler's natural urge to play will kindle learning. It makes the body strong, stimulates the mind, and strengthens confidence and social skills. It helps to diffuse stress. It fosters social-emotional resilience. It is not surprising that experts in child psychology look at play to enhance child development.

How do you inject play and fun into your preschooler's schedule?

Encourage your child to get physical.

Get your child to dance, sing, swing, hop, climb, do somersaults, jump, and hop or stand on one leg.

Physical movement prevents obesity and develops motor skills. It builds confidence. Going down a playground slide, for example, allows your child to take risks in a safe environment. It gives him the thrill and wonderment of discovering what he is capable of doing. Physical play makes for a happy, healthy, and confident child.

Arrange playdates.

Playdates give opportunities for play and social interaction. They teach your child to take turns and to share. They help your child develop social skills and build friendships.

Use games and humor.

A child tends to want to do things when he sees them as fun. Turn a task into a game, and you will have a child eager to do what you ask him to.

One mom shares how she was able to turn things around. Instead of nagging her stubborn child to get him to put on his shoes for school, she would play shoe store with him. Speaking with a silly accent, she'd say, "Good morning, sir! Welcome to Mom's Shoe Store. The shoes you ordered just arrived. Would you like to try them on?" It never fails to get her child all excited to put on his shoes.

Prioritize free play.

Children spend a considerable part of their day engaged in supervised and structured activities. Encourage your child to use his imagination and to develop creativity by giving him time for free play. Give him play dough, paint and paper, a huge used box, clothes to play dress-up with, and similar items, and tell him to "Go play."

Unstructured or free play is also called playful learning. It nurtures curiosity, imagination, and creativity, which should all be part of high-quality preschool education.

Turn on the music.

Cheerful tunes work magic. Turn on some music, and suddenly it becomes more fun to do things. If you are low in creativity, you can simply suggest 'racing' against a tune. "Do you think you can change into your pajamas before they finish singing 'The Wheels on the Bus'?"

Use everyday objects to multitask as toys.

Inexpensive, everyday simple objects help support creativity. Children have been known to find wooden spoons, empty containers, puzzles, blocks, and other fascinating items.

Encourage pretend-play.

Playing 'pretend' or make-believe with your preschooler is both fun and educational. It encourages the use of imagination and language.

Encourage the use of imagination by having your child act out imaginary roles or scenes. Read a book with your child and use the story as a basis for pretend play. Merging pretend games with reality by playing house while your child helps you with household chores.

Chapter 10:
The Importance of Warmth and Affection

When parenting a child of any age, including a child going through the tough years between 2 and 5 years of age, keep one essential thing in mind. Your effectiveness as a parent is fundamentally dependent on the quality of your relationship with your child.

Preschool teachers point out that when a teacher has positive feelings of warmth and affection towards a child, that child will likely enjoy life-long positive results from the interaction.

A child who grows up under the influence of a warm, nurturing, and supportive adult shows high self-esteem, good communication skills, improved academic performance, with fewer behavior and socio-emotional problems. On the other hand, a child who does not enjoy the same warm and friendly nurturing tends to suffer from low self-esteem and to feel vulnerable, insecure, unworthy, and socially unskilled.

20. Show your child affection and encouragement.

Encourage and love your child, and you will have one who grows up to be strong, well-adjusted, and resilient. The strong foundation you give him by loving him enables him to stay strong and hopeful amid adversity.

Talk and listen to your child. Teach him. Reassure him that you love him while you discipline him. Show him acceptance and stability.

Show your appreciation for the little things that he does for you. Praise him for his effort to do what is right.

Show that you understand and respect him. Include him in simple family discussions. Show him that his opinions and feelings count.

Do not smother him. Respect his individuality. Defer to his present individual comfort level and make adjustments as this level changes through the years.

Spend time with your child. Play games. Do fun things with him. Be silly with him. Create happy memories with him.

As you take the time to be truly present in your child's life, you assure him that he can depend on you and that you love him. You release him from worrying about adult-sized problems. You give him space to be the kid that he is. When you make your preschooler feel loved and secure, you set him free to learn, have fun, and be creative.

Conclusion

The period between the ages of 2 and 5 years is critical for your child's growth and development. It is a vital and decisive time for setting the foundation for his transition from baby and toddler to becoming a 'little person.' It helps him prepare for continuing learning, cognitive development, language development, school success, and emotional and social competence.

As a parent, you are given the beautiful gift of playing a unique role in your child's life. I hope the tips presented in this book -- 20 simple, practical, tried-and-tested techniques used by successful preschool teachers over the years, will inspire you, encourage you, and help make the job of parenting your preschool-aged child easier, more meaningful, and incredibly fulfilling!

Thank you for reading this book. I wish you the best of luck!